aaaaaaaaaaaalice by Jennifer Karmin
published by flim forum press
www.flimforum.com
cover art by Felicia Leach
printed by Boyd Printing Company, Albany, NY
ISBN 978-0-9790888-3-4

aaaaaaa

aaaalice

You can be trying to connect the experience of being lost with something external or physical, but we are really connecting what is experienced with what is experienced.

Mei-mei Berssenbrugge

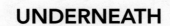

UNDERNEATH

even if my head would go through

rain for rent

the liquor store
has milk
for $1.99
extra large eggs
for 99¢

enjoy the sport
of country club
living

freeway entrance
vs. thruway
or expressway

your shoes are
weird

that store sells
donuts and chinese food

self serve
church of christ
meets here

cattle for sale

**it would be
of very little use
without
my shoulders**

we've reached

the point

where

we understand

we've reached

the

point where

we understand a little

we've reached the

point where we

understand

a little

these days

it used to be

difficult

but we've

reached the

point where we

understand a little these days

at the beginning
it was difficult
but we've reached
the point where we
understand a little
these days

yes but i grow at a reasonable pace

ok
rub your
thumb and index
finger together

not sure
shrug your
shoulders

good luck
keep your
fingers crossed

be quiet
put your
finger on your
lips

to be angry
poke your
finger

you may
also try
to beckon
just a moment
thumbs up
thumbs down

**not
in that
ridiculous fashion**

it's

never high

it's not very

high

it's not a

bit high

it's

not at all

high

it's not

especially high

it's

really not high

it's ordinarily not

high

it's
not
so
high
we'll
probably
be amazed

you might

sandwiches
taste better
when they are
cut diagonally
feed the
mayonnaise
to the tuna

        knock

it's april
now it's april
again
the dog still
looks up   **and**

in a dream
dad says
you are dead too

woulda
coulda
shoulda   **i**

no
moe doesn't say
ouch

                  could

let
you
out

instead of

        nails

                      we used

          screws

                            instead

     of milk

we

            used water

instead of hot

       water

                     we used

     cold water

                     instead of gas we

     used electricity

         instead
         of nothing
         we had
         everything

THRUWAY

then

keep your feet
moving

buy apple juice

you   stand outside
what it feels like
to not be

on a bus

wonder where
all the roads
go

when your period
will come again

watch a man
walk his dog

should   say hello
to the girl
who says
hello
to everybody

what's your name
she asks the old man
with cowboy boots
red baseball cap
going to reno

my name's peter
like peter rabbit

say what you mean

it's different

depending on the

year

it's

different depending

on the day

it's different

depending

on the time

it's different

depending

on the

place

it's different depending

on the person

it's different

depending

on

the thing

it's different depending on the

weather

it's different depending

on it's different

it's
different
depending
on
us

i'm not particular as to size

feet smell
noses run
writing as
a way of
life

you lose head
from your heat

you lose heat
from your head

wake up
can't find shoes
or notebook

greenriver is
the watermelon
capital of the world

to look different
to have a
bigger smile

**only one
doesn't like
changing
so often
you know**

we

waited until

the car

got old

we waited

until
the movie began

we

waited until the ship

went out

we waited until a

friend came

we waited
until
everyone
stood up

everybody has won

children playing
drive with
care

have exact
fare ready

escalator
out of use

please
deposit
litter in
baskets

beware
bags look
alike

all seats
bookable
in advance

we regret
any inconvenience

**and
all must
have prizes**

a

        round one

                              or

                square one

                                      a thin

                        one

or thick

       one

                                        a low one

                              or

         high one

                                    a dark one or

             light one

                this one
                    or
                that one

consider my dear

things
to learn
and why

see
a schoolhouse
built in 1910

writing as
practice
everyday

how to
give love

if you can't
go over
go under

chaos
is always
apparent

some people say
curious things

yesterday
a man was walking

how many
thoughts a day
we write

hear silence
sound of close eyes

she is only a child

we don't

        remember

                             we

            don't remember

  for sure

    we don't remember

       how many

                       years

    it comes

                to

      we've already

forgotten

        how many years

                     it

  comes to

we don't know how

          many years

      it comes to

        we can't
        tell
        how many
        years
        it comes
        to

besides that's not a regular rule

nagasaki
atom bomb
epicenter

boys
ride
bicycles

around and
around and
around

you

one boy drops
his juice
stops his bicycle
quick
to pick it up

they
run
and chase
each other

invented

a girl with
two plastic bottles
sings
makes music

waves
at grandma

it

who sits
watching her play
here

just now

it

would be

better

to buy it

in advance

it would be

better

to turn it

off

it would

be better to

fix it

it would be better to

quit it

it would

be better to

forget it

it would
be better
to learn it

i've had nothing yet

a sway
of bamboo
in the wind

like they would
fall over
don't appear
so strong
but green   **so**

where am
or where going
or how to
get there

not sure
if it is
past or future

sun on back
familiar
good morning   **i**

could be going
anywhere
in any part
of life

amazed
by kindness   **can't**

take
more

we

stay home

we stay

home

looking after

the children

and so

on

we stay

home

watching the house

and looking

after

the children and so

on

we always
stay
home
and so on

PRACTICE

that's the reason they're called lessons

hands sticky
thumb nails
stained

two small
mikan

oranges
gifts from
two kid friends
they are seven

laugh
and tell them
you are
seven
too

listen
for words
to understand

why to sign
your name
on their father's
petition

why the government
wants to move
the town cemetery
their dead families

reverse the conversation
how was your day
what did you do
where are you from

**because they lessen
from day to day**

singing

songs

and making

a racket

eating and

drinking

swimming and taking

walks

raining and

snowing

being hot

and

being cold

going on and

off

coming and going

going out

and coming in

tasting

good and tasting

awful

sometimes
understanding
and sometimes
not understanding

take care of the sense

underground tunnels
strangeness
of war

a place
where 175
japanese men
killed themselves

after
americans smiled
held babies
gave out chocolates

okinawa is
blue green ocean
comfort of water

middle
of night
sleep
stops

hot
sunburn
go for
a walk
tranquil
in a dream

feeling of
somewhere
totally
unknown

**and the sounds
will take care
of themselves**

we wish

                                      it had

                            rained

                                                    we wish

              it

                                  had come early

  we

                      wish it

            had been

                                                            interesting

                          we wish it

                had been near

                                              we wish

it had been simple

                              we wish it

                had gone

                                  we wish
                                  it had
                                  been a wish

if that's all you know about it

no problem
no relationship

no want
don't want

have
don't have

don't
understand

just
looking

hot
water
beautiful
sorry

where
is

excuse
me

good
bye
wait

**you may
stand down**

tell

                    us

           to try

                  asking

tell us

              to continue

                      tell

us to send

              it soon

tell us to

                    go for a

           walk

                      tell us

to check it

              tell us to lock

                it

            tell
            us
            to
            do
            it

ORANGES

that depends

top bunk
overnight train

hard to
sit up   **a**

loud
awake
announcement
music
movement

open window
sun rising
people fishing

china slow
7 am

hot water
makes steam
makes tea   **good**

the baby with
the pink knit hat
has lost
her shoe

the man on
the bottom bunk
communicates   **deal**
where eyes
meet

**on where
you want
to get to**

by

all means

we want to

go

and see

at any rate

we

want to

go and see

after this

we want to go

and see

that is why we

want

to go

and see

now
we
want
to go and see

the best way

call home
try to answer

what do you
see right now

a female officer
riding her bicycle
with a red umbrella

to   eating ice cream

adolescent boys whistling
through their fingers
eating watermelon

people shaking
fortune sticks

explain   at the temple
good luck

sit
still

almost
not wanting
to write

it

is to do it

it's

a large

room

it's a

quiet room

it's

a strange

room

it's a fine

room

it's

a noisy room

it's

a

small room

it's a clean

room

it's
our
room

i've read that in some book

laughter
is

to
let
go

a process
replace
with
instinct

put feet
in a cold stream
near a waterfall
listen

can't depend
on places
even language

to have space
to walk

in fulung
the life guard reports
the ocean is
too angry
for swimming

at dusk
the bus driver
gestures
no charge

but i don't
remember where

we're

           thinking of

                    going

tonight

      we're thinking

    of going

              out

      tonight

we're

           thinking of stopping

in tonight

               we're thinking of

going home

            tonight

    we're thinking

        of going

home

          early tonight

we're thinking of going to

      bed early tonight

    we're
    thinking
    early tonight

ANNOUNCEMENT

the game's going on

people
trees
fields

rhythm of
a cobblestone
road

himalayan
mountains

ni hao
hello
to everyone

going to
or coming from

it's market
day

women carry
big baskets
on their backs

children run
in a field
try to catch
butterflies

words
and
wind

**rather better
now**

thanks

for the

letter

thanks for

the interesting

book

thanks

for the telephone

call

thanks for the

newspaper

thanks for

the delicious

candy

thanks for waiting

thanks

for listening

thanks for looking

for it

thanks

for remembering it

thanks
for
the time

but it's no use

don't know
what day
it is

only hills
and yaks
handwriting
in notebook

bus packed
with tibetans
and muslims

the monk
sitting behind
hands out
small green apples

arrive
in the middle
of a snowstorm

look forward
to sleep
signs of
what's next

**because
i was
a different person
then**

going

back

to

yesterday

we plan

to

do it

we plan

to

do it when

we have free

time

we

plan to

do it since

we came

all the way

we plan to do it

since

we took

the trouble

we
plan
to do it
in the future

i almost think

please
come in

                         i

a surprise

smells
yak butter
candles burning

teenage monks

whisper   **can**
giggle
run out
warm up

all colors

hold spirits

                       remember

conscious
of permission

wanting to
see   **feeling**

a little
different

there's

really

a lot

of snow

there's too

much

snow

there's

an amazing amount

of snow

there's an awful lot of

snow

there's
awfully
pretty
snow

WIND

then you keep moving round

teach
the hokey pokey
in exchange
for a handful
of nuts

melt down
scrap metal
tin cans

make a pot
to cook
dinner with

turn
prayer
wheels

help them go
where prayers go

top of the
mountain
sky burial

tibetans
cut up
the body

ask vultures
to eat it
carry it off

scattered
bones and clothes

karma to finish

i suppose

we'll be

there

with lunch

we'll

be there

with

the tickets

we'll be there

with the

estimate

we'll

be there with

the letter

we'll be there

with

the key

we'll be there with

the

map

we'll be there
with the answer

there's a great deal

hike
without
sun
for a new year

uphill
chest hurts
pounding but high

climb
until fire
throw papers
make a wish   **to**

your new friend proclaims
we didn't think
it was possible
to have family
in america

smoke
in the sky   **come**
circle
the ground
again

before that

please

deliver the

paper

as early

as possible

please stop

the car

as near as

possible

please

draw the map

as

big as possible

please
define
this
as
simply
as
possible

at least i know

lesha serves
chocolate chip cakes
apple pies
green tea
huge bowls of
yak milk yogurt

who

murmurs
no good no good

cut her long hair
to wear earrings
a white muslim hat

marriage at sixteen
a man
she did not know

i

tibetan becomes
chinese becomes
english

was

lesha's niece
chanting
hello mimi
hello mimi

when i got up
this morning

it matters

whether

we go

or

not

it

matters whether

we

want to go

or not

it matters whether

we use it

or

not

it matters
whether
we write
it or
not

HANDFUL

call it

are
you
enough

stop and go
train motion

a young chinese
couple

secret of
communication

he points to
a phrase book

jittering

nervous

she wrings
her hands

trying to
remember and speak

what you like

four

                                                    is twice

                                    two

                three is

                                    three
        times one

                                    twelve is six

                        times two

                                    twenty
        is four times

                                                    five

                fifty is five

                                                            times

                        ten

                                    one
                                    hundred
                                    is
                                    ten
                                    times
                                    ten

i don't believe there's

rush hour
bicycle traffic
in beijing

too late
the taoist temple
is closed

an

wander to
a department store

buy
a new pen

consumerism
is world culture

atom

hear english
you have
a beautiful nose

like
a store
in any country

of

except
third floor indoor
ice skating rink

someone
slowly gliding

**meaning
in it**

we will

                                talk
        it over

                        we
would have
                                        talked

                it over
                        we would

                                                like
        to talk it

                                        over
        we think

                        we will

        talk it over

                        we want to

                        talk
        it over

                        let's talk
                        it
                        over

some

snow
absence of color
calm spaces

get off
here
ulan bator   **of**

a yurt
is a tent
made of felt

on horseback
genghis khan created
the mongolian empire
korea to hungary

step outside   **the**
for five minutes

go inside
let hands thaw
continue strolling

gandan monastery
only monastery
to surivive the 1930s
soviet purges

death and celebration   **words**
combined

have got
altered

it's

a place

of interest

it's a famous

place

it's a

pretty place

it's

a place with

a nice

view

it's a warm

place

it's a

new place

it's
a special
place

ENOUGH

i mean

vladimir declares
he is
the best poet
in siberia

was sent
for three years
as a dissident

stayed now
twenty-two years

having just arrived
today
tell him
he is the only poet
you know
in siberia

flick of light
in his eyes
he motions big arms

shouts poetry
walt whitman
in russian

mystery
why lake baikal
does not freeze
when everything
else does

winter has come early
no one expected it

what i say

we

need

to leave

within

a week

we need

to

leave next

week

we need to

leave

by saturday

we

need

to leave on the

tenth

we need to leave before

the month is

over

we need
to leave
soon

i think i may as well

stumble outside
to the toilet
early morning

soundless
dark
but stars

burn fingers
on the stove door
trying to throw
toilet paper in

didn't know
it would be
so hot

even
touch it again

feel blister
red smoothness
the hot burned in

numb
at the same
time

**go in
at once**

                                        things

    like planting

                        trees

                                    and weeding

        things like

                        repairing

                                            old houses

    and

                putting up

                                    new houses

        things like going

                    fishing

                                        and taking walks

                                    things like
                                    studying
                                    language
                                    and reading

it means much

landscape is
part of life
days continue

set up home
trans-siberian railway

liza comes to talk
grandmother follows
smile gold teeth
many questions
for usa

liza in high school
likes nirvana and metallica
english is fun
proudly shows pictures
a soldier boyfriend
he lives in moscow
is twenty-one

passengers happy
two or three times
a day
the train stops

purchase
fresh brown bread
red wine
warm potatoes

take photos
crunch snow
crisp air
deep breaths

the same thing

once in

a

while we

go

together

we

sometimes go together

we often

go

together

we

usually go together

we ordinarily go

together

we go together

a good

deal

we go

together almost

everyday

we
always go
together

LAKE

how are you

a quiet man
shares the compartment

turns away
as he changes
his shirt

outside keeps
moving

                                                  getting

reading a newspaper
see numbers
tattooed
on his arm

he is an engineer
has two children
resembles an older
clint eastwood

his name
is very hard   **on**
to pronounce

pause
stutter

every time
you try
to say it

                                                        now

my
dear

before

the nails

come out

let's

fix it

before it goes

bad

let's fix

it

before it

breaks

let's

fix it

before it collapses

let's

fix it

before it
falls
let's fix
it

i'm never sure

want
something in words
what it means

what

can't see
the rabbi

women sit
separate
from men
behind
a screen

i'm

a jewish synagogue
in moscow

going

graffiti near the kremlin
the guide translates
get out kykes

to

holes of
family

grandpa's reply
to his russian childhood

be

it was not easy
for us

from one minute
to another

in case

we're

in a hurry

in

case we

want

to ask a

question

in case we

can't hear

in

case we

feel rain

in case

we go home

early

in case
we
don't
understand

thank you sir

unlike
memory

golden
more mystical

visiting
historical churches

hands sometimes
look like buddha's

mary seems sad
by the announcement

she is to be
the mother
of god

her baby
a miniature man

his body grows
hips tilted
legs slightly crossed
half naked

imagine a taste
of salt and blood

**for your
interesting story**

what

a strange

way

of walking

what a

strange

way of

talking

what a strange

way

of looking

what

a strange way

of reading

what a strange way

of writing

what
a strange
way of
thinking

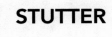

STUTTER

and what is the use

before religion
government
country
was people

handmade
objects

ethnography museum
st. petersburg

mass production
gives
leisure time

one
narrative

frustration
grasping with language
living seeing knowing
not able to obtain

myths we
create

without
pictures or
conversations

of

a

book

please

             rope

         that

                      rope

that rope

                      please

        please lift

pull that

please hold

please lower

tie that rope

that rope

please
let go
of that
rope

oh

i've

had

such

a

curious

dream

leaving
no closure

open what
is inside

matryoshka
a russian toy
to teach children
nothing is ever
what it seems

a smiling woman
another
and another

search
for the smallest
tiniest self

uncover
what is
underneath

take all
the people

carry them
inside

find
what is
home

we've reached

we've reached the point where we understand

we've reached the point where

it used to be difficult

the beginning it was difficult but we're reached

the point where we understand

a little

we understand a little these days

but we've reached the point where we understan

the point where we understand a little these da

These poems are a word score for polyvocal improvisation. Performers are encouraged to equate the style of each text with imagined tones, rhythms, voices, etc. Any number of performers may participate and any number of pages may be used.

Werner Heisenberg's uncertainty principle states that it is impossible to determine both the exact position and momentum of a subatomic particle. Conceiving of words as atoms, every reading of this text-sound epic should produce new results. The sequence and time relations of the words create unlimited permutations intended for reading, sound, and performance experiments.

Collage texts were derived from two invaluable sources:

Alice's Adventures in Wonderland by Lewis Carroll
(Signet Classic, 1960)

Beginning Japanese Part 2 by Eleanor Harz Jorden and Hamako Ito Chaplin
(Yale University Press, 1963)

for Dad
we say hello

in memory of
Perry Saul Karmin

Time and place: I moved to Japan in 1996. In the fall of 1998, I began a three month solo journey through Taiwan, China, Tibet, Mongolia, Siberia, and Russia.

Big thanks and gratitude for birthing the book: Elizabeth Cross, Matthew Goulish, Aaron Karmin, Beth Nugent, Dai Sato, and You.

The utmost appreciation and love to Kath Duffy for inspiration and making the best bowl of popcorn ever.

I am deeply indebted to editors Adam Golaski and Matthew Klane for their encouragement and creative vision. A selection of these poems was first published in *A Sing Economy* (Flim Forum Press, 2008).

Thanks and thanks for ongoing help and faith: Charles Bernstein, Amina Cain, Teresa Carmody, David Emanuel, Ken Feltges, Goat Island Performance Group, Dan Godston, Mama Haha, Susan Howe, Mike Hynes, Lisa Janssen, Dan Mejia, Mom, Vanessa Place, Tim Roche, Beth Snyder, Chuck Stebelton, the Dusie Kollektiv, the Poetics Program at SUNY Buffalo, and the Writing Program at the School of the Art Institute of Chicago. Especially: comrades, collaborators, teachers, students, and fellow travelers in Chicago, Buffalo, Portland, and Japan.

The development of this project was supported by Community Arts Assistance Program grants from the City of Chicago Department of Cultural Affairs and the Illinois Arts Council.